omelettes & frittatas

omelettes & frittatas

Jennie Shapter   photography by Tara Fisher

RYLAND
PETERS
& SMALL

LONDON NEW YORK

First published in Great Britain in 2005
by Ryland Peters & Small
20–21 Jockey's Fields
London WC1R 4BW
www.rylandpeters.com

10 9 8 7 6 5 4 3 2 1

ISBN 1 84172 817 9

A CIP record for this book is available from the British Library.

Senior Designer Steve Painter
Commissioning Editor
    Elsa Petersen-Schepelern
Production Sheila Smith
Art Director Gabriella Le Grazie
Publishing Director Alison Starling

Food Stylist Jennie Shapter
Stylist Paul Hopper

Notes

• All spoon measurements are level unless otherwise specified.
• All eggs are medium or large, as specified. Uncooked or partly cooked eggs should not be served to the very young, the very old, those with compromised immune systems or to pregnant women.

Author's note

Unfortunately eggs are susceptible to salmonella and as a safeguard it is recommended that we eat only eggs that are well cooked and have no trace of softness. Salmonella is not present in all eggs and, while it must be taken very seriously, I am still prepared to accept the slight risk of a soft, creamy middle in the centre of my own omelettes, but the decision is yours.

However, as a general rule, people at risk, such as the elderly, the very young, pregnant women and anyone recovering from a serious illness, should be aware and avoid French-style omelettes (see note left). Tortillas and frittatas are fine, but double check that they are completely cooked in the centre before serving.

contents

6 breakfast or brunch …
8 omelette know-how
10 omelettes
28 italian frittatas
44 spanish tortillas
64 index

breakfast or brunch,
lunch or a light supper …

Is there anyone who doesn't enjoy a well-made omelette? The light and airy French omelette is one of the quickest of all meals An Italian frittata or Spanish tortilla may take a little longer, but the process is much more relaxed, leaving you time to chat or sip a glass of wine. Frittatas and tortillas are also easier to make when serving several people. These flat omelettes are extremely versatile, served hot or cold as snacks, for main meals, light lunch or supper dishes, for picnics or even between chunks of crusty bread.

Where possible, buy free-range or organic eggs with bright yellow yolks. Buy the very best quality and, above all, make sure the eggs are fresh. The flavour of the omelette will be affected by the quality of the eggs.

Many of the French omelette recipes have been written for one person or two to three for a snack or light meal, while the tortillas serve two, four or even more people. It is difficult to be exact, as it all depends on when you are serving them and how big an appetite you have. If you have any leftover tortilla or frittata, it can be eaten cold the next day, although I find the plate always seems to end up empty, no matter the number of servings.

omelette know-how

Choosing the right equipment

Omelettes are easy to make, but it is essential to use the right equipment. One of the secrets of a good omelette is the pan. Regardless of the type of omelette you are making, the size, shape and material from which the pan is made are extremely important and, ideally, you should keep that pan exclusively for omelette making.

A French omelette pan has a curved edge, which makes it easier to turn the omelette out onto the plate. For a tortilla or frittata, a large frying pan with sloping sides is best.

Choose a heavy-based pan, either cast iron, aluminium or non-stick – everyone has their favourite. If you choose cast iron or aluminium, it must be well seasoned first, otherwise the eggs will stick. A non-stick pan solves this problem, but you must use non-scratch tools to avoid damaging the surface. Whichever you choose, it must have a heavy base, because a thin base doesn't disperse the heat evenly. Avoid stainless steel; though attractive, it is not a good conductor of heat.

To season a pan, follow the instructions supplied with the pan. If there aren't any, fill it with about 1 cm depth of cooking oil and heat gently until hot, reduce to a low heat for about 30 minutes, then let cool. Repeat, then discard the oil and wipe off any excess with kitchen paper.

Some omelettes, such as soufflés, oven-baked ones, tortillas and frittatas, are finished under the grill or in the oven, so it is essential to use a pan with a heatproof or removable handle. Remember that the handle will be hot, so make sure you hold it with an oven glove.

The size of the pan is equally important – too small and the omelette will be too thick and will not fold, too large and the eggs will be thin and leathery. I have given a guideline of pan sizes for small (18 cm), medium (20–21 cm) and large (24 cm) in the recipes, but these can be varied slightly by about a centimetre either way. It is important to measure the base of the pan, not the top, as is often quoted on the packaging of a new pan.

Making the omelette …

All cooks have their favourite omelette-cooking method. The first decision is the choice of cooking medium – oil or unsalted butter. Whichever you choose, make sure you heat it gently and swirl it around the base and the sides of the pan before adding the eggs, to stop them sticking. For French omelettes, I like to use butter or a combination of butter and sunflower oil. Butter imparts a rich flavour, but will burn easily, so be careful – adding a little oil will help. For tortillas and frittatas, oil is more common – either extra virgin olive oil or sunflower oil. Again, your preference for flavour will probably dictate which you use. I prefer olive oil to impart a flavour in recipes such as the classic potato tortilla where the potatoes almost stew in the oil.

French omelettes should be made quickly, drawing the egg mixture from the edges to the centre, until the eggs are cooked but still creamy in the middle. Preferred utensils include the back or flat of a fork or a tablespoon, though a spatula or palette knife can also be used.

Use the spatula to loosen the edges of a tortilla or frittata before turning or removing from the pan. To finish cooking a tortilla, you should turn it over in the pan, so you will need a large, flat plate or saucepan lid. Shake the pan to check that the tortilla is not stuck to the bottom before setting the plate or lid over the top of the pan. Hold the pan with one hand and the plate or lid with the other. Turn both over together so the tortilla drops onto the plate. Use the spatula to help ease the tortilla back into the pan.

Pan care

If your pan is seasoned aluminum or cast iron, don't wash it after cooking an omelette. After each use, wipe it well with a damp cloth or kitchen paper. If anything should stick to the pan, rub it off with kitchen paper dipped in a little salt.

The mixture

The success of a good omelette is often in the correct mixing of the eggs. Break them up with a fork, rather than beating fiercely with a whisk, which would make the eggs too liquid, spoil their texture and produce a heavy, leathery omelette. Under- rather than over-beating is the secret of success.

Herbs will taste even better if you pick them just before cooking, so if you grow your own, this is the perfect omelette for you. You can vary them to suit what you have available, just make sure that if you include powerful varieties like sage or mint, use less, while more subtle types such as chervil can be increased.

summer herb omelette

3 large eggs

1 tablespoon snipped fresh chives

2 tablespoons chopped fresh dill

1 tablespoon chopped fresh tarragon

2 teaspoons unsalted butter

fresh herbs such as chives and chive flowers or a handful of basil, to serve

sea salt and freshly ground black pepper

an 18-cm heavy omelette pan (measure the base, not the top)

serves 1

Break the eggs into a bowl and season with a little salt and pepper. Whisk briefly with a fork, just enough to mix the yolks and whites. Mix in the chives, dill and tarragon.

Melt the butter in the omelette pan over medium-high heat and swirl it around to coat the bottom and sides of the pan. When the butter starts to foam, pour in the eggs.

Using a spatula or back of a fork, draw the mixture from the sides to the centre as it sets. Let the liquid flow and fill the space at the sides and, at the same time, tip the pan backwards and forwards.

After a short time, the omelette will be cooked but still creamy in the centre. Tilt the pan and fold over a third of the omelette towards the centre, then fold over again, slide onto a warmed plate and serve immediately with extra herbs.

Variations

Cheese omelette Omit the herbs and add 2 tablespoons grated Cheddar cheese. Sprinkle 1 tablespoon grated cheese over the omelette before folding.

Mushroom omelette Omit the herbs. Before making the omelette, chop about 50 g mushrooms and cook them gently in a little oil or butter for about 10 minutes, until all the excess moisture has evaporated. Sprinkle over the omelette before folding.

omelettes

A strong blue cheese such as Roquefort adds a powerful flavour to this omelette, which I love. However if you prefer a more delicate flavour, try using smooth, creamy-textured dolcelatte, or a mountain Gorgonzola. Both these cheeses are quite soft and will not crumble like Roquefort, so are best chopped into small pieces before adding.

caramelized onion and blue cheese omelette

1 tablespoon unsalted butter

1 tablespoon sunflower oil

1 small onion, halved and thinly sliced

3 large eggs

40 g blue cheese such as Roquefort, crumbled

sea salt and freshly ground black pepper

an 18-cm heavy omelette pan (measure the base, not the top)

serves 1

Put half the butter and oil in the omelette pan and heat until the butter has melted. Add the onion and fry gently for about 10 minutes, until golden and caramelized, stirring occasionally.

Meanwhile, break the eggs into a bowl and whisk briefly with a fork, just enough to mix the yolks and whites. Season with salt and pepper. Using a slotted spoon, add the onions to the eggs and mix gently.

Increase the heat to medium-high and add the remaining butter and oil if necessary. When the pan is hot, pour in the omelette mixture. Using a spatula or back of a fork, draw the mixture from the sides to the centre as it sets. Let the liquid flow and fill the space at the sides.

Sprinkle the cheese over the top, fold over a third of the omelette to the centre, then fold over the remaining third. Slide onto a warmed plate and serve immediately.

It is important to start folding the omelette while it is still slightly liquid in the centre to avoid it over-cooking and becoming tough and leathery. Make sure the person who is going to eat it is ready first, rather than the omelette.

smoked salmon omelette

75 g smoked salmon, cut into thin strips

1 tablespoon milk

3 large eggs

2 teaspoons unsalted butter

2 tablespoons crème fraîche

1 tablespoon chopped fresh dill

sea salt and freshly ground black pepper

an 18-cm heavy omelette pan (measure the base, not the top)

serves 1

Put half the smoked salmon in a bowl, add the milk and let stand for 15 minutes.

Break the eggs into a bowl whisk briefly with a fork, just enough to mix the yolks and whites. Season with salt and plenty of pepper, then stir in the milk and smoked salmon.

Heat the butter in the omelette pan. When the butter starts to foam, pour in the egg mixture and cook over medium-high heat, drawing the mixture from the sides to the centre as it sets. Let the liquid flow and fill the space at the sides.

After a short time, the omelette will be cooked but still creamy in the centre. Top the omelette with the crème fraîche and sprinkle with chopped dill and the remaining smoked salmon.

Fold over a third of the omelette to the centre, then fold over the remaining third, slide onto a warmed plate and serve immediately.

Variation This omelette can also be made with 2 large eggs, using a 15-cm omelette pan.

There is nothing quite like the flavour of fresh crab, but if it isn't available, use frozen crabmeat. Make sure you drain it well before adding to the omelette. This recipe would work equally well with peeled prawns.

oriental crab omelette

3 large eggs

1 teaspoon Thai fish sauce or soy sauce

freshly ground black pepper

1 tablespoon chopped fresh coriander

50 g white crabmeat, fresh or frozen and thawed

5 teaspoons sunflower oil

1 small chilli, deseeded and chopped

3 spring onions, finely sliced

an 18 cm heavy omelette pan (measure the base, not the top)

serves 1

Break the eggs into a bowl and whisk briefly with a fork, just enough to mix the yolks and whites. Stir in the fish sauce and season with pepper. Mix the coriander and crabmeat in a bowl and set aside

Heat 1 tablespoon of the oil in the omelette pan, add the chilli and three-quarters of the spring onions, then stir-fry for 1 minute. Remove from the pan with a slotted spoon and stir into the eggs.

Add the remaining oil to the pan, heat for a few seconds, then pour in the egg mixture. Tip the pan to spread the eggs evenly over the base, leave for 5 seconds, then draw the edges of the omelette to the centre, letting the liquid egg flow to the sides and at the same time tipping the pan backwards and forwards.

After a short time, the omelette will be cooked but still creamy in the centre. Sprinkle the coriander and crabmeat mixture over the omelette. Tilt the pan, fold one-third of the omelette towards the centre, then fold over again and transfer to a warmed plate. Serve immediately sprinkled with the remaining spring onions.

Ideal for a lunch or supper dish, or perfect for al fresco dining served with a crisp salad, this omelette is just bursting with flavour. It is worth buying tomatoes ripened on the vine for their extra taste explosion.

feta cheese and tomato open omelette

5 large eggs

2 tablespoons chopped fresh basil

1 tablespoon chopped fresh mint

3 spring onions, finely chopped

2 tablespoons sunflower oil

75 g feta cheese, crumbled

8 small cherry tomatoes, halved

sea salt and freshly ground black pepper

an 18-cm heavy omelette pan (measure the base, not the top)

serves 2

Break the eggs into a bowl and whisk briefly with a fork, just enough to mix the yolks and whites. Season with salt and pepper, add 2 tablespoons water, the basil, mint and spring onions and mix briefly.

Heat the oil in the omelette pan. Pour in the egg mixture and cook over medium heat for 4–5 minutes, drawing the mixture from the sides to the centre until the omelette is half cooked.

Top with the feta and the tomato halves, cut side up, and cook for 2 minutes. Slide under a preheated grill and cook until light golden brown. Slide onto a warmed plate and serve immediately.

A fusion of tortilla-inspired wraps with Portuguese-style piri-piri chicken. Piri-piri is a hot sauce made from serrano chillies; increase or reduce the amount of sauce in the marinade depending on how hot you would like it.

omelette wraps

2 tablespoons extra virgin olive oil

freshly squeezed juice of 1 lime

2 tablespoons chopped fresh coriander

1 tablespoon piri-piri sauce, or other hot sauce such as harissa

2 skinless chicken breasts, about 150 g each, cut into thin strips

5 medium eggs

2 tablespoons milk

2 tablespoons finely snipped fresh chives

1 avocado, halved, pitted, peeled and chopped

6 cherry tomatoes, quartered

4 teaspoons unsalted butter

sea salt and freshly ground black pepper

a non-stick frying pan

an 18-cm heavy omelette pan (measure the base, not the top)

serves 2

Put the olive oil, lime juice and coriander in a bowl and mix with a fork. Put half the mixture in a shallow dish, add the piri-piri sauce and mix well. Add the chicken and stir to coat with the marinade. Set aside for 30 minutes.

Break the eggs into a bowl, then add the milk, salt and pepper. Whisk briefly with a fork, just enough to mix the yolks and whites. Mix in the chives. Add the avocado, cherry tomatoes, the remaining olive oil and lime juice and stir gently to coat.

Stir-fry the chicken in a non-stick frying pan for 3–4 minutes, or until the juices run clear, then remove from the heat and set aside.

Meanwhile melt half the butter in the omelette pan over medium-high heat and swirl it around to coat the bottom and sides of the pan. When the butter starts to foam, pour in half the eggs.

Tip the pan to spread the eggs evenly over the base, leave for 5 seconds, then draw the edges of the eggs to the centre, letting the liquid egg flow to the sides. When the omelette has just set, transfer to a warm plate, add the remaining butter to the pan and cook the second omelette in the same way.

Mix the cooked chicken with the avocado and tomatoes and divide between the two omelettes, spooning the mixture in a line down the middle. Roll up the omelettes, cut in half and serve.

A soufflé omelette is quite simple to prepare and results in an amazingly light and fluffy dish that just melts in the mouth. This one is finished with Taleggio cheese, which oozes out of the centre as you cut into it.

cheese and watercress soufflé omelette

4 large eggs, separated

50 g mature Cheddar cheese, grated

25 g watercress, chopped

50 g Taleggio cheese

2 tablespoons unsalted butter

1 small red onion, finely chopped

2 tablespoons freshly grated Parmesan cheese

sea salt and freshly ground black pepper

an 18-cm heavy frying pan (measure the base, not the top)

serves 2

Put the egg yolks in a large bowl, add the grated Cheddar, watercress, salt and pepper and mix well. Cut the Taleggio into thin slices, then in half crossways.

Put the frying pan over medium heat. Melt half the butter in the pan, add the onion and cook for 4–5 minutes, or until softened. Remove with a slotted spoon and stir into the egg yolk mixture. Preheat the grill to the highest setting.

Put the egg whites in a very clean bowl and whisk until soft peaks form. Fold into the egg yolk mixture. Add the remaining butter to the pan, increase the heat to medium-high and, as soon as the butter is foaming, pile the omelette mixture into the pan and gently shake it to even out the mixture. Cook for 2 minutes, or until pale gold on the underside.

Top with the Taleggio and slide under the preheated grill to melt the cheese and finish cooking the top of the omelette. Fold in half, transfer to a warmed plate and serve immediately, sprinkled with the Parmesan.

4 large eggs

2 tablespoons plain yoghurt

1 teaspoon ground cumin

2 tablespoons chopped
fresh coriander

1 garlic clove, crushed

2 tablespoons sunflower oil

1 onion, finely chopped

1 small red chilli,
deseeded and chopped

3 cm piece of fresh ginger,
peeled and grated

2 tomatoes, finely chopped

sea salt and freshly
ground black pepper

cucumber raita

about 8-cm cucumber, peeled

150 g plain yoghurt

2 spring onions, finely chopped

1 tablespoon chopped
fresh coriander

1 teaspoon freshly squeezed
lime juice

sea salt and freshly
ground black pepper

*an 18-cm heavy omelette pan
(measure the base, not the top)*

serves 2–3

Eggs, while not particularly common in Indian cooking, are adored by the Parsee community of Bombay, especially when made into a spicy, aromatic omelette. It is served like a Spanish omelette, hot or cold, cut into wedges, often with chutney or a raita on the side. I like this cool cucumber raita because it complements the delicious spicy flavours of ginger and chilli.

indian omelette

To make the cucumber raita, coarsely grate the cucumber and squeeze out the excess moisture. Put in a bowl, then stir in the yoghurt, spring onions, coriander, lime juice, salt and pepper. Chill.

To make the omelette, break the eggs into a bowl, add the yoghurt and whisk briefly with a fork, just enough to mix the yolks and whites. Stir in the cumin, coriander, garlic, salt and pepper.

Heat 1 tablespoon of the oil in the omelette pan. Add the onion, chilli and ginger and fry over medium-high heat for 2–3 minutes, then add the tomatoes and cook for 1–2 minutes. Using a slotted spoon, transfer to the egg mixture and stir gently.

Add the remaining oil to the pan and swirl it around to coat the bottom and sides. Pour the egg mixture into the pan, reduce the heat to low and cook for about 5–6 minutes, or until the underside is golden and the top has almost set.

Slide under a preheated grill to finish cooking or put a plate over the top of the pan and invert so the omelette falls onto the plate. Slide back into the pan and cook for 1–2 minutes. Cut into wedges and serve with a spoonful of raita.

This is a great way to cook an omelette – once prepared, it can finish cooking in the oven, making the whole thing quite relaxed. It is ideal for a late, lazy breakfast, but good enough to eat at any time of the day. Make sure the pan handle is ovenproof or removable.

baked brunch omelette

2 tablespoons sunflower oil

4 slices smoked bacon, cut into strips

1 onion, finely sliced

1 medium potato, cubed

75 g button mushrooms, sliced

5 large eggs

90 ml milk

75 g mature Cheddar cheese, grated

1 tablespoon unsalted butter

1 tablespoon freshly grated Parmesan cheese

sea salt and freshly ground black pepper

a 20-cm heavy non-stick frying pan (measure the base, not the top)

serves 2–3

Preheat the oven to 200°C (400°F) Gas 6. Heat the oil in the frying pan, add the bacon, onion and potato and fry for 6 minutes, or until the potatoes start to brown. Add the mushrooms and fry for 2 minutes.

Meanwhile put the eggs and milk in a large bowl and whisk briefly with a fork, just enough to mix the yolks and whites. Season with salt and plenty of pepper. Stir in three-quarters of the Cheddar.

Using a slotted spoon, transfer the potato mixture to the bowl of eggs and mix well. Add the butter to the frying pan and, when it starts to foam, pour in the omelette mixture. Sprinkle with the remaining cheese and transfer to the preheated oven.

Cook for 12–15 minutes, or until just set. Loosen the edges with a spatula or palette knife and slide onto a warmed serving plate. Sprinkle with Parmesan and serve immediately.

Porcini are difficult to buy fresh, but are widely available
dried. They are one of the best mushrooms, with an
intense, rich flavour that will pervade the omelette. Strain
the soaking liquid from the porcini and add a spoonful
to the omelette mixture, or keep it for a soup or stew.

porcini frittata

15 g dried porcini mushrooms

6 medium eggs

3 tablespoons
mascarpone cheese

3 tablespoons chopped
fresh flat leaf parsley

3 tablespoons extra virgin olive
or sunflower oil

1 onion, halved and sliced

125 g button mushrooms, sliced

1 tablespoon freshly grated
Parmesan cheese

1 tablespoon unsalted butter

75 g fresh wild mushrooms

sea salt and freshly
ground black pepper

a 20-cm heavy
non-stick frying pan
(measure the base, not the top)

serves 2–3

Put the porcini in a small bowl and cover with warm water. Let soak
for 30 minutes. Break 1 of the eggs into a bowl, add the mascarpone
and mix well. Add the remaining eggs and whisk briefly with a fork.
Stir in the parsley and season with salt and pepper.

Heat 1 tablespoon of the oil in the frying pan, add the onion and
cook over low heat until soft. Add another tablespoon of oil and
the mushrooms and cook for 5 minutes. Drain the porcini and
chop if large. Add to the pan and cook for 2 minutes.

Using a slotted spoon, transfer the mushrooms and onions to the
eggs and mix gently.

Wipe out the frying pan with kitchen paper, add the remaining oil
and heat gently. Add the frittata mixture and cook over low heat
until browned on the underside and nearly set on top. Sprinkle
with Parmesan and slide under a preheated grill to finish cooking
the top and melt the cheese. Transfer to a warm serving plate.

Melt the butter in the frying pan, add the wild mushrooms and
sauté quickly. Spoon over the top of the frittata and serve.

Baby spinach is essential for this recipe because the leaves wilt and soften quickly, so you needn't remove the stalks or chop the leaves. The pancetta adds a special depth of flavour. Like all frittatas, this one is wonderful to take on a picnic or serve in a packed lunch.

spinach and pancetta frittata

6 large eggs

1 tablespoon extra virgin olive or sunflower oil

125 g smoked pancetta, cut into cubes, or smoked bacon lardons

4 spring onions, chopped

1 garlic clove, finely chopped

175 g baby spinach

sea salt and freshly ground black pepper

a 24-cm heavy frying pan (measure the base, not the top)

serves 4

Break the eggs into a bowl and whisk briefly with a fork. Season well with salt and plenty of pepper.

Heat 1 tablespoon of the oil in the frying pan. Add the pancetta or bacon pieces and cook over medium heat for 3–4 minutes until they start to brown.

Add the spring onions, garlic and spinach and stir-fry for 3–4 minutes or until the spinach has wilted and the onions have softened.

Pour the egg mixture into the pan, quickly mix into the other ingredients and stop stirring. Reduce to a low heat and cook for 8–10 minutes, or until the top has almost set. Slide under a preheated grill to finish cooking the top. Serve hot or cold, cut into wedges.

This frittata has a real Mediterranean feel and is flavoured with some of Italy's favourite ingredients – olives, sun-dried tomatoes and Parmesan cheese. If you have the time, it is worth mixing the tomatoes and sage into the eggs up to an hour before cooking for a more intense flavour.

sun-dried tomato and parmesan frittata

6 large eggs

8 sun-dried tomatoes in oil, drained and sliced

1 tablespoon chopped fresh sage leaves

50 g pitted black olives, thickly sliced

50 g freshly grated Parmesan cheese, plus extra shavings to serve (optional)

2 tablespoons extra virgin olive oil

1 onion, halved and sliced

sea salt and freshly ground black pepper

a 20-cm non-stick frying pan (measure the base, not the top)

serves 2–3

Break the eggs into a large bowl and whisk briefly with a fork. Add the sun-dried tomatoes, sage, olives, Parmesan, salt and pepper and mix gently.

Heat the oil in the frying pan, add the onion and cook over low heat until soft and golden.

Increase the heat to moderate, pour the egg mixture into the pan and stir just long enough to mix in the onion. Cook over medium-low heat until the base of the frittata is golden and the top has almost set.

Slide the pan under a preheated grill to finish cooking or put a plate or flat saucepan lid on top of the pan and invert the pan so the frittata drops onto the plate or lid. Return the frittata to the pan, cooked side up, and cook on top of the stove for 1–2 minutes.

Transfer to a serving plate, top with Parmesan shavings, if using, and serve hot or cold, cut into wedges.

The frittata is Italy's version of a flat, open-faced omelette and this one is simply flavoured with fresh mint and courgettes. The courgettes can be coarsely grated rather than sliced, but make sure you squeeze out any excess water first before adding to the frying pan.

minted courgette frittata

6 large eggs

2 tablespoons chopped fresh mint

250 g baby new potatoes, thickly sliced

2 tablespoons extra virgin olive or sunflower oil

1 large onion, chopped

4 courgettes, sliced

sea salt and freshly ground black pepper

a 24-cm heavy frying pan (measure the base, not the top)

serves 3–4

Break the eggs into a bowl and whisk briefly with a fork. Season well with salt and pepper. Mix in the chopped mint.

Cook the potatoes in a saucepan of boiling, salted water until just tender. Drain thoroughly.

Meanwhile, heat the oil in the frying pan, add the onion and cook gently for about 10 minutes, until soft and pale golden. Add the courgettes and stir over low heat for 3–4 minutes until just softened. Add the potatoes and mix gently.

Pour the eggs over the vegetables and cook over low heat until the frittata is lightly browned underneath and has almost set on top. Slide under a preheated grill for 30–60 seconds, to set the top. Serve, cut into wedges.

Pecorino is the generic name for all Italian cheeses made from sheep's milk. Pecorino Romano from Lazio, the region around Rome, is one of the best known and probably Italy's oldest cheese. It has a sharp, dry flavour and a hard texture, perfect for grating, which makes it the best choice for this recipe.

asparagus, pecorino and prosciutto frittata

6 asparagus spears, about 100 g, cut into short lengths

250 g frozen broad beans or peas, thawed

6 large eggs

75 g freshly grated pecorino cheese

3 tablespoons chopped fresh oregano

1 tablespoon chopped fresh flat leaf parsley

2 tablespoons extra virgin olive or sunflower oil

1 medium onion, chopped

3 thin slices Parma ham, or other prosciutto

sea salt and freshly ground black pepper

a 24-cm heavy non-stick frying pan (measure the base, not the top)

serves 3–4

Put the asparagus in a saucepan of boiling water and cook for about 5 6 minutes, or until just tender. Refresh in cold running water and drain thoroughly. If using broad beans, remove the waxy skins and discard.

Break the eggs into a large bowl and whisk briefly with a fork. Season with salt and pepper and mix in two-thirds of the cheese, all the oregano, parsley, asparagus and broad beans or peas.

Heat the oil in the frying pan, add the onion and cook over medium heat for 5 minutes, or until just starting to brown. Pour the frittata mixture into the pan and briefly stir in the onion. Reduce the heat to low and cook for 12–15 minutes, or until the frittata is golden brown underneath and almost set on top.

Sprinkle with the remaining pecorino. Tear the Parma ham slices into 2–3 pieces and arrange on top of the frittata. Slide under a preheated grill for 2–3 minutes to melt the cheese and frizzle the ham. Loosen the edges with a spatula and slide onto a warm plate.

A frittata should be cooked slowly, only lightly coloured and still slightly moist when served. The Italians usually flip it to finish cooking, but often a recipe will suggest quickly flashing the frittata under the grill or putting it in a hot oven just to set the top. I prefer the grill, but use whichever method you find easiest.

char-grilled pepper frittata

1 small red pepper,
quartered and deseeded

1 small yellow pepper,
quartered and deseeded

1 small green pepper,
quartered and deseeded

2 tablespoons ricotta or
mascarpone cheese

6 large eggs

2 tablespoons fresh thyme leaves

2 tablespoons extra virgin olive
or sunflower oil

1 large red onion, sliced

1 tablespoon balsamic vinegar

2 garlic cloves, crushed

sea salt and freshly
ground black pepper

a 20-cm heavy frying pan
(measure the base, not the top)

serves 2–3

Put the peppers skin side up under a preheated grill and cook until the skins have blackened. Transfer to a bowl, cover and let cool. This will steam off the skins, making them easier to remove.

Put the cheese in a large bowl, add 1 egg and mix to loosen the cheese. Whisk in the remaining eggs with a fork. Season with salt, pepper and thyme and stir into the cheese mixture.

Peel the blackened skins off the peppers and rinse under cold running water. Pat dry with paper towels and cut into thick strips. Stir into the bowl.

Heat half the oil in the frying pan, add the sliced onion and balsamic vinegar and cook over gentle heat for about 10 minutes until softened. Add the garlic and cook for 1 minute.

Using a slotted spoon, add the onion to the egg mixture and stir. Add the remaining oil to the pan and heat gently. Pour the frittata mixture into the pan and let cook over low heat until almost set, puffy and light golden-brown on the underside.

Finish under a preheated grill or put a plate or flat saucepan lid on top of the pan and invert the pan so the frittata drops onto the plate or lid. Slide back into the pan and cook for 30–60 seconds. Transfer to a serving plate and serve hot or at room temperature, cut into wedges.

250 g broccoli, trimmed

6 large eggs

3 tablespoons extra virgin olive oil

1 large onion, chopped

1 garlic clove, crushed

1 red chilli, deseeded and finely chopped

125 g cooked peeled prawns, cut into pieces if large

75 g mozzarella cheese, cubed

sea salt and freshly ground black pepper

Parmesan shavings, to serve (optional)

pesto sauce

50 g basil leaves

1 garlic clove, chopped

2 tablespoons pine nuts

5 tablespoons freshly grated Parmesan cheese

125 ml extra virgin olive oil

sea salt and freshly ground black pepper

a 24-cm heavy non-stick frying pan (measure the base, not the top)

serves 3–4

Basil, with its intense spicy scent and pungent sweet flavour, is a cornerstone of Mediterranean cooking, and is the main ingredient for pesto sauce. You can use ready-made pesto, but it really is worth a little extra effort to make it yourself and capture the redolence of the fresh herb.

mozzarella and prawn frittata with pesto

To make the pesto sauce, put the basil leaves in a blender or food processor, add the garlic, pine nuts, grated Parmesan, olive oil, salt and pepper and blend until creamy. Set aside.

Cut the broccoli into small florets, put in a saucepan of boiling, salted water and cook until barely tender. Drain and refresh under cold running water, then drain again thoroughly.

Break the eggs into a bowl, add salt and pepper, whisk briefly with a fork and set aside. Heat the oil in the frying pan, add the onion and cook for 5 minutes, stirring frequently. Add the garlic and chilli and fry for 2 minutes, stirring frequently. Stir in the broccoli and prawns.

Pour the egg mixture into the pan, making sure it reaches the edges. Dot the cubes of mozzarella over the top. Cook over low heat until almost set, then slide under a preheated grill for 1–2 minutes, until the top has set and the cheese is bubbling. Let cool slightly, then cut into wedges. Trickle pesto sauce over the top, add the Parmesan shavings, if using, and serve.

This classic tortilla consists of just three ingredients: eggs, potatoes and onions. Together, they are transformed into an unbelievably delicious dish. Tortillas may be cut into squares or wedges and eaten for lunch or supper, as a snack or for a picnic, or even between chunks of bread – a favourite way in Spain. You can also cut it into smaller squares and serve it as tapas with drinks.

classic spanish tortilla

1 large onion

3–4 tablespoons extra virgin olive or sunflower oil

4 medium peeled potatoes, about 500 g, peeled

5 large eggs

sea salt and freshly ground black pepper

a 20-cm heavy non-stick frying pan (measure the base, not the top)

serves 2–3

Cut the onion in half, then slice thinly lengthways and separate into slivers. Heat 3 tablespoons of the oil in the frying pan.

Thinly slice the potatoes, then add them to the pan in layers, alternating with the onion. Cook for 10–15 minutes over medium-low heat, lifting and turning occasionally, until just tender. The potatoes and onions should not brown very much.

Meanwhile, break the eggs into a large bowl, whisk briefly with a fork and season with salt and pepper. Remove the potatoes and onions from the pan and drain in a colander, reserving any oil. Add the vegetables to the bowl of eggs and mix gently.

Heat the reserved oil in the pan, adding a little extra if necessary. Add the potato and egg mixture, spreading it evenly in the pan. Cook over medium-low heat until the bottom is golden brown and the top almost set.

Put a plate or flat saucepan lid on top of the pan and invert the pan so the tortilla drops onto the plate or lid. Return to the pan, brown side up, and cook on top of the stove for 2–3 minutes until the other side is lightly browned. Turn again and transfer to a serving plate, with the most attractive side upward. Serve hot or at room temperature, cut into wedges.

spanish tortillas

A robust omelette packed full of goodness, this is a perfect recipe for using up small quantities of leftover vegetables, including ingredients such as broccoli, corn, broad beans or mushrooms. I like to finish this tortilla under the grill to retain the lovely colours on the top when serving, but you can also turn it over in the pan to finish cooking in the classic way.

hearty country-style tortilla

4 tablespoons extra virgin olive or sunflower oil

3 medium potatoes, about 325 g, peeled and cubed

1 onion, halved and sliced

75 g green beans, trimmed and cut into three

4 asparagus spears, cut into 5-cm lengths

1 red pepper, quartered, deseeded and thinly sliced

75 g spicy chorizo, sliced

1 garlic clove, finely chopped

6 large eggs

75 g frozen peas

sea salt and freshly ground black pepper

a 24-cm heavy non-stick frying pan (measure the base, not the top)

serves 4–6

Heat 2 tablespoons of the oil in the frying pan. Add the potatoes and cook over medium heat for 5 minutes. Add the onion and cook for 10 minutes or until the potatoes are almost tender, lifting and turning occasionally.

Meanwhile put the beans and asparagus in a saucepan of boiling, salted water and cook for 5 minutes. Drain and refresh in cold water. Drain well.

Add the pepper, chorizo, asparagus, beans and garlic to the potatoes and cook for 5 minutes, stirring frequently.

Break the eggs into a large bowl, add salt and pepper and whisk briefly with a fork. Mix in the peas and cooked vegetable mixture.

If necessary, wipe out the frying pan with kitchen paper, then add the remaining oil and heat until hot. Add the tortilla mixture, letting it spread evenly in the pan.

Cook over medium-low heat for about 10 minutes until the bottom is golden brown and the top almost set. Slide under a preheated grill to set and lightly brown the top. Transfer to a serving plate and serve hot or warm, cut into wedges.

A speciality of the Alicante region of Valencia is an unusual meat paella finished with an omelette topping. For this mouth-watering tortilla, I have replaced the meat with the shellfish typical of Paella Valenciana.

paella tortilla

3 tablespoons extra virgin olive or sunflower oil

1 skinless chicken breast, about 175 g, cut into strips

1 onion, chopped

1 garlic clove, chopped

1 red pepper, halved, deseeded and sliced

2 tomatoes, chopped

100 g short grain Spanish rice, such as calasparra

a pinch of saffron threads, soaked in 2 tablespoons hot water

250 ml chicken stock

150 g mixed seafood, such as prawns, mussels and squid rings

6 medium eggs

3 tablespoons frozen peas, thawed

sea salt and freshly ground black pepper

a 24-cm heavy non-stick frying pan (measure the base, not the top)

serves 4–6

Heat 2 tablespoons of the oil in the frying pan, add the chicken and fry until browned. Transfer to a plate.

Add the onion, garlic and red pepper and fry for 5–6 minutes, stirring frequently, until softened.

Stir in the tomatoes, rice and saffron and pour in the stock. Add the chicken and season with salt and plenty of black pepper. Cover and cook over gentle heat for about 20 minutes, or until the rice is almost tender, adding a little more stock if necessary.

Stir in the mixed seafood and cook for 5 minutes, or until the rice is just tender and all the liquid has been absorbed.

Break the eggs into a large bowl, add salt and pepper and whisk briefly with a fork. Stir in the paella mixture and the peas.

Wipe out the pan with kitchen paper. Heat the remaining oil in the pan over medium heat. Add the tortilla mixture and cook over medium-low heat for 10–15 minutes, or until almost set.

Slide under a preheated grill to set the top. Let stand for 5 minutes, then transfer to a serving plate and serve, cut into wedges.

Note If ready-mixed seafood cocktail is unavailable, use 50 g each of shelled prawns, shelled mussels and squid rings.

Although potato is the traditional ingredient in a Spanish omelette, chickpeas are a delicious alternative, adding a slightly sweet, nutty flavour. This tortilla is quite filling, so is best as a main meal; I like to serve it with a crisp green salad and a glass of red wine.

chickpea tortilla

5 large eggs

½ teaspoon sweet oak-smoked Spanish paprika

3 tablespoons chopped fresh flat leaf parsley

3 tablespoons extra virgin olive oil

1 large onion, finely chopped

I red pepper, halved, deseeded and chopped

2 garlic cloves, finely chopped

400 g canned chickpeas, rinsed and well drained

sea salt and freshly ground black pepper

a 20-cm heavy non-stick frying pan (measure the base, not the top)

serves 2–3

Break the eggs into a large bowl, add salt, pepper and paprika and whisk briefly with a fork. Stir in the chopped parsley.

Heat 2 tablespoons of the oil in the frying pan. Add the onion and red pepper and cook for about 5 minutes until softened, turning frequently. Add the garlic and chickpeas and cook for 2 minutes.

Transfer to the bowl of eggs and stir gently. Add the remaining oil to the pan and return to the heat. Add the chickpea mixture, spreading it evenly in the pan. Cook over medium-low heat until the bottom is golden brown and the top almost set.

Put a plate or flat saucepan lid on top of the pan and hold it in place. Invert the pan so the tortilla drops onto the plate or lid. Slide back into the pan, brown side up, and cook for another 2–3 minutes until lightly browned on the other side. Serve hot or at room temperature, cut into wedges.

Most tortillas are inverted onto a plate and returned to the pan to finish cooking. However, this tortilla is topped with cured mountain ham and should be finished under the grill. You can trickle a little extra virgin olive oil over the top before grilling and, for a truly extravagant touch, add a few slices of goats' cheese log such as Soignon Petite Sainte-Maure, which melts beautifully into the top of the tortilla.

tortilla with artichokes and serrano ham

3 tablespoons extra virgin olive or sunflower oil

3 medium potatoes, about 350 g, peeled and cubed

1 Spanish onion, chopped

5 large eggs

400 g canned artichoke hearts in water, well drained and cut in half

2 tablespoons fresh thyme leaves

100 g thinly sliced serrano ham, torn into strips

6–8 slices goats' cheese log with rind, about 125 g (optional)

sea salt and freshly ground black pepper

a 24-cm heavy non-stick frying pan (measure the base, not the top)

serves 3–4

Heat 2 tablespoons of the oil in the frying pan. Add the potatoes and cook over medium heat for 5 minutes. Add the onion and cook for a further 10 minutes, lifting and turning occasionally, until just tender. The potatoes and onions should not brown very much.

Meanwhile, break the eggs into a large bowl, season with salt and pepper and whisk briefly with a fork.

Add the artichokes, thyme and about three-quarters of the ham to the bowl of eggs. Add the potatoes and onion and stir gently.

Heat the remaining oil in the frying pan. Add the tortilla mixture, spreading it evenly in the pan. Cook over medium-low heat for about 6 minutes, then top with the remaining ham. Cook for a further 4–5 minutes or until the bottom is golden brown and the top almost set.

Add the goats' cheese, if using, and slide under a preheated grill just to brown the top, about 2–3 minutes. Serve hot or warm, cut into wedges.

Buy deep orange sweet potatoes to achieve the best effect for this colourful tortilla. To melt the Brie, the tortilla is finished in the oven, so use a pan with a heatproof handle.

sweet potato and brie tortilla

2 medium sweet potatoes, about 500 g, peeled and cut into chunks

4 tablespoons extra virgin olive or sunflower oil

1 onion, halved lengthways and sliced about 5 mm thick

5 large eggs

1 garlic clove, crushed

125 g Brie cheese

sea salt and freshly ground black pepper

a shallow roasting tray

a 20-cm heavy ovenproof frying pan (measure the base, not the top)

serves 2–3

Put the potatoes and 2 tablespoons of the oil in the roasting tray and toss to coat. Roast in a preheated oven at 200°C (400°F) Gas 6 for 15 minutes, then add the onion and mix well. Roast for a further 20 minutes, or until all the vegetables are tender.

Break the eggs into a large bowl and whisk briefly with a fork. Stir in the salt, pepper and garlic. Add the potatoes and onions and mix gently.

Heat the remaining oil in the frying pan. Pour the tortilla mixture into the pan and cook over medium-low heat for 6–8 minutes, or until it has set around the edges and is lightly browned underneath.

Slice the Brie and arrange on top of the tortilla. Return to the oven for 5 minutes, or until the Brie has melted and the top of the tortilla has set. Serve hot or warm, cut into wedges.

There are many variations of Eggah served throughout the Middle East, but Persian (Iranian) cuisine provides one of the finest. The flavour from copious quantities of fresh herbs bursts out as you bite into it. I like to add nuts for their interesting texture – if you have time, lightly toast the pine nuts first for a more intense flavour.

persian herb eggah

3 tablespoons sunflower oil

1 onion, chopped

1 small aubergine, halved and sliced

1 garlic clove, crushed

5 large eggs

5 tablespoons chopped fresh flat leaf parsley

5 tablespoons chopped fresh coriander

3 tablespoons chopped fresh dill

2 tablespoons chopped walnuts

1 tablespoon pine nuts

5 green cardamom pods, crushed, the black seeds retained and the pods discarded

sea salt and freshly ground black pepper

a 20-cm heavy non-stick frying pan (measure the base, not the top)

serves 2–3

Heat 2 tablespoons of the oil in the frying pan. Add the onion and cook for about 5 minutes, turning frequently, until beginning to soften. Add the aubergine and cook with the onion for another 5 minutes. Stir in the garlic and cook for 1 minute.

Meanwhile, break the eggs into a large bowl and whisk briefly with a fork. Mix in the parsley, coriander, dill, walnuts, pine nuts, black seeds from the cardamom pods, a little salt and plenty of pepper. Remove the onion and aubergine from the pan with a slotted spoon and add to the egg mixture. Stir well.

Add the remaining oil to the pan and return to the heat. Add the tortilla mixture, spreading it evenly in the pan. Cook over medium-low heat until the bottom is golden brown and the top almost set.

Put a plate or flat saucepan lid on top of the pan and invert the pan so the tortilla drops onto the plate or lid. Slide back into the pan, brown side up, and cook for 2–3 minutes until lightly browned. Serve hot or at room temperature, cut into wedges.

Loaded with sausages, fried potatoes and onions, this dish is perfect comfort food. Ring the changes with different kinds of sausage – try slices of chorizo, cubes of black pudding or morcilla (traditionally Spanish), spicy Italian sausages or even frankfurters.

sausage, potato and onion tortilla

3–4 tablespoons extra virgin olive or sunflower oil

6 pork chipolata sausages with herbs

1 onion

3 medium potatoes, about 325 g, thinly sliced

5 large eggs

sea salt and freshly ground black pepper

a 20-cm heavy non-stick frying pan (measure the base, not the top)

serves 2–3

Heat 1 tablespoon of the oil in the frying pan. Add the sausages and fry for 8–10 minutes, turning them frequently. Remove and set aside. Wipe out the pan with kitchen paper.

Cut the onion in half and then into slivers lengthways.

Heat 2 tablespoons of the oil in the cleaned pan. Add the potatoes, layering them with the onions. Cook for 10–15 minutes over medium-low heat, lifting and turning occasionally, until just tender. The potatoes and onions should not brown very much.

Meanwhile, break the eggs into a large bowl, add salt and pepper and whisk briefly with a fork. Remove the potatoes and onions from the pan with a slotted spoon and add to the egg mixture. Thickly slice the sausages and mix with the eggs and potatoes.

Return the frying pan to the heat, adding a little more oil if necessary. Add the potato and egg mixture spreading it evenly. Cook over medium-low heat until the bottom is golden brown and the top has almost set.

Put a plate or flat saucepan lid on top of the pan and invert the pan so the tortilla drops onto the plate or lid. Slide back into the pan, brown side up, and cook for 2–3 minutes until lightly browned underneath. Serve hot or warm, cut into wedges.

There is nothing quite like the char-grilled flavour of roasted vegetables; as a tortilla filling they make a delicious alternative to the more traditional potato. You can roast the vegetables up to 24 hours in advance and keep chilled until you are ready to make the tortilla. Allow a little extra time to cook the tortilla because the vegetables will be cold.

roasted vegetable tortilla

1 red onion, cut into wedges

1 red pepper, deseeded and cut into thick strips

1 leek, thickly sliced

1 gem squash, peeled, deseeded and diced, or about 125 g butternut squash or pattypans, cut into cubes

6 sprigs of thyme

2 garlic cloves, unpeeled

3 tablespoons extra virgin olive or sunflower oil

6 large eggs

sea salt and freshly ground black pepper

a roasting tin

a 24-cm heavy non-stick frying pan (measure the base, not the top)

serves 3–4

Put the onion, red pepper, leek and squash in large roasting pan. Sprinkle with thyme, salt and pepper, bury the garlic cloves under the vegetables and sprinkle with 2 tablespoons of the oil. Roast in a preheated oven at 200°C (400°F) Gas 6 for 20 minutes, then turn the vegetables over and roast for a further 10 minutes.

Remove from the oven and let cool for 5 minutes. Remove the soft flesh from the roasted garlic and discard the skins. Discard the thyme stalks, removing any leaves still attached.

Break the eggs into a large bowl, add salt and pepper and whisk briefly with a fork. Add the vegetables and mix gently.

Heat the remaining oil in the frying pan. Add the tortilla mixture and cook over medium-low heat for about 10 minutes or until the bottom is golden brown and the top almost set.

Put a plate or flat saucepan lid on top of the pan and invert the pan so the tortilla drops onto the plate or lid. Return it to the pan, browned side up, and cook for 2–3 minutes until lightly browned underneath. Alternatively, slide under a preheated grill to finish cooking the top. Let stand for 5 minutes to settle. Serve hot or at room temperature, cut into wedges.

index

a
artichokes, tortilla with, and serrano ham, 55
asparagus, pecorino and prosciutto frittata, 39

b
baked brunch omelette, 26

c
caramelized onion and blue cheese omelette, 13
char-grilled pepper frittata, 40
cheese:
  asparagus, pecorino and prosciutto frittata, 39
  cheese and watercress soufflé omelette, 22
  cheese omelette, 10
  caramelized onion and blue cheese omelette, 13
  feta cheese and tomato open omelette, 18
  sun-dried tomato and parmesan frittata, 35
  sweet potato and brie tortilla, 56
chickpea tortilla, 52
classic spanish tortilla, 44
courgette, minted, frittata, 36
crab, oriental, omelette, 17

e
eggah, persian herb, 59

f
feta cheese and tomato open omelette, 18
free-range eggs, 4, 7
frittatas, 28–43
  asparagus, pecorino and prosciutto, 39
  char-grilled pepper, 40
  minted courgette, 36
  mozzarella and prawn, with pesto, 43
  porcini frittata, 31
  spaghetti and rocket, 28
  spinach and pancetta, 32
  sun-dried tomato and parmesan, 35

h
hearty country-style tortilla, 47
herbs:
  minted courgette frittata, 36
  persian herb eggah, 59
  summer herb omelette, 10

i
indian omelette, 25
italian frittatas, 28–43

m
mixing eggs, 9
mozzarella and prawn frittata with pesto, 43
mushrooms:
  mushroom and pepper tortilla tapas, 48
  mushroom omelette, 10
  porcini frittata, 31

o
organic eggs, 4, 7
oriental crab omelette, 17
omelette wraps, 21
omelettes, 10–27
  baked brunch, 26
  caramelized onion and blue cheese, 13
  cheese and watercress soufflé, 22
  feta cheese and tomato open, 18
  indian, 25
  oriental crab, 17
  smoked salmon omelette, 14
  summer herb, 10
  wraps, 21
onion:
  caramelized, and blue cheese omelette, 13
  potato, sausage and, tortilla, 60

p
paella tortilla, 51
pan care, 9
pancetta, spinach and, frittata, 32
pans, 8–9

pesto, mozzarella and prawn frittata with, 43
pepper:
  char-grilled, frittata, 40
  mushroom and, tortilla tapas, 48
persian herb eggah, 59
porcini frittata, 31
potato:
  classic spanish tortilla, 44
  sausage, and onion tortilla, 60
prawn, mozzarella and, frittata with pesto, 43
prosciutto, asparagus, pecorino and, frittata, 39

r
roasted vegetable tortilla, 63
rocket, spaghetti and, frittata, 28

s
salmonella, 4
sausage, potato and onion tortilla, 60
seasoning pans, 9
serrano ham, tortilla with artichokes and, 55
smoked salmon omelette, 14
soufflé omelette, cheese and watercress, 22
spaghetti and rocket frittata, 28
spanish tortillas, 44–63
  chickpea tortilla, 52
  classic spanish tortilla, 44
  hearty country-style tortilla, 47
  mushroom and pepper tortilla tapas, 48
  paella tortilla, 51
  roasted vegetable tortilla, 63
  sausage, potato and onion tortilla, 60
  sweet potato and brie tortilla, 56
spinach and pancetta frittata, 32

summer herb omelette, 10
sun-dried tomato and parmesan frittata, 35
sweet potato and brie tortilla, 56

t
tapas, mushroom and pepper tortilla, 48
tomato:
  feta cheese and, open omelette, 18
  sun-dried, and parmesan frittata, 35
tortillas, 44–63
  chickpea tortilla, 52
  classic spanish tortilla, 44
  hearty country-style tortilla, 47
  mushroom and pepper tortilla tapas, 48
  paella tortilla, 51
  roasted vegetable tortilla, 63
  sausage, potato and onion tortilla, 60
  sweet potato and brie tortilla, 56
  with artichokes and serrano ham, 55

w
watercress, cheese and, soufflé omelette, 22
wraps, omelette, 21